Memory Lane

Cleethorpes

Evening Telegraph

Memory Lane
Cleethorpes

STUART RUSSELL

The Breedon Books
Publishing Company
Derby

First published in Great Britain by
The Breedon Books Publishing Company Limited
Breedon House, 44 Friar Gate, Derby, DE1 1DA.
1999

ISBN 1 85983 164 8

Printed and bound by Butler & Tanner Ltd., Selwood Printing Works,
Caxton Road, Frome, Somerset.

Colour separations by GreenShires Ltd, Leicester.

Jackets printed by Lawrence-Allen, Avon.

Contents

Foreword

We stand on the verge of a new age.

As the year 2000 approaches it brings for all of us new hopes and aspirations.

But as we look ahead to what the future may hold in store it is also time to reflect on what has gone before. For our heritage is also a part of our future.

Over one hundred years ago the *Grimsby Evening Telegraph* made its first appearance and over the ensuing decades has been a cornerstone of the local community, recording in words and pictures the events that helped shape the day-to-day lives of ordinary people.

This book looks back on that remarkable century.

The pictures which tell Cleethorpes' story are from the *Evening Telegraph's* own

archives, the majority of them taken by the newspaper's photographic staff.

Here you will find recollections of events that touched the lives of everyone. For this is a book not only about a town, but also about its people.

It is a tribute to past memories, some happy, some sad, but all of them fascinating.

I hope you enjoy your trip with us down Memory Lane.

PETER MOORE
Editor
Evening Telegraph

Introduction

Two hundred years ago Cleethorpes welcomed the first visitors who would lay down the foundations for its future development. The beginnings were modest, but were soon enhanced with the arrival of steam packet services to the River Humber which in the 1820s, 30s and 40s brought in people from an increasingly wide area. They liked what they saw.

Then came the railway, which connected Grimsby with other parts of the country. The age of the day tripper had arrived. But those who made the journey in the early days found little to entertain them. Eventually, things began to change, and a pier was opened in 1873 and in 1886 the Manchester, Sheffield and Lincolnshire Railway Company, which by then had taken over the seafront, created and opened a promenade and pleasure gardens.

Cleethorpes was growing up – so much so that by 1881, 230,000 ordinary and 72,000 excursion passengers visited the resort.

The 1920s saw further expansion with part of the seafront which had hitherto been used as golf links, being developed and a boating lake and bathing pool built there. In 1935 the then urban district council bought back the pier, promenade and gardens from what had become the London and North Eastern Railway.

More modern times have seen the creation of a thriving holiday town, which, because of its short summer season is also an attractive and increasingly popular place in which to live.

This book is a tribute to Cleethorpes and the people who have made it the place it is today. It is a record of 100 years in the life of a town, a trip down Memory Lane which will evoke memories both happy and sad.

Welcome to Cleethorpes and the way we were.

A Walk on the Prom

For the thousands of visitors who poured from the trains which brought them from the industrial areas of Yorkshire, the Pier and North Promenade were the first ports of call on their day by the sea. They were lured to Cleethorpes with newspaper and poster advertising and through copies of the resort's brochure, pages from which are featured here.

Right: Flying high. A gull's eye view of the sea front made an attractive invitation to the resort.

Far Right: Fresh air and fun. The ingredients which made Cleethorpes a special place for the visitors who came from some of the heavy industrial areas.

Wonderful Wonderland. It proudly boasted to be the largest covered amusement park on the east coast. And with its host of attractions it proved an all-day venue for many holidaymakers.

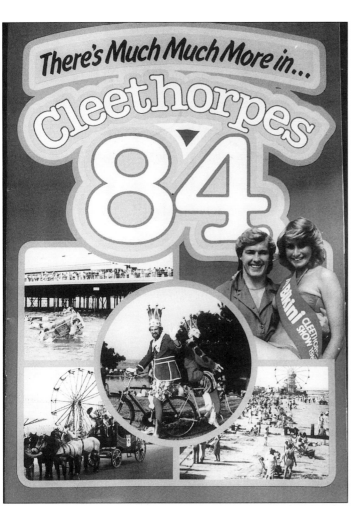

There was much more to enjoy in Cleethorpes according to this copy of the holiday guide. The cover featured Chris Quentin, better known as *Coronation Street's* Brian Tilsley.

There's lots to do – how the resort was advertised on posters in 1953.

This was how we told the country about Cleethorpes in 1983.

A poster advertising Cleethorpes in 1951 featured the resort's famous donkeys.

9

A fine old picture of Cleethorpes Pier. It is believed to have been taken in 1900.

One way of seeing the sights was in this boat on wheels. The date is not known.

Disaster. Fire destroyed the Pier Pavilion in July 1903. This picture was taken by Mr Fred Garton, of Hull, who worked as 'boots' at the Dolphin Hotel for many years.

A view of old Cleethorpes taken from a picture postcard. The date is not known.

The way it was. A shot of the Pier Pavilion taken in 1903 and one of the few surviving pictures of the old structure.

A low flying Hurricane fighter from the Battle of Britain Flight is pictured over the Pier in July 1982.

The War Office declared its own 'war' on Cleethorpes Pier following the outbreak of hostilities in 1939 – it cut the structure in two, marooning the café which had replaced the old pavilion at the far end. But during the war the café itself caught fire and was destroyed. Following the war the pier stub was demolished by the War Department. In this picture, taken in April 1949, the remaining piles are being blown up with gelignite. The *Evening Telegraph* reported: 'For 70 years the old pier had given enjoyment to thousands of visitors. In new spheres its component parts will continue to help give pleasure. Most of the 200 tons of salvaged timber decking is being used in the rebuilding of Leicester City FC's war blitzed grandstand.' Steel girders and other timber was used in building work at Wonderland.

The scene from the beach in 1949 as part of the Pier was demolished.

In the beginning… the Pier as it was on February 28, 1874.

Seafront attractions in about 1910.

Fun on the sands in the early years of the century.

Picture postcard views of a growing resort.

The seafront and 'flying machine' in the early 1900s.

'New Dips' says
the sign at the
top of the Big
Dipper tower.
The year was
1974.

An advertisement proclaims 'It's quicker by rail' in this old shot of the entrance to the Pier Gardens.

Visitors were few when this picture was taken. Admission to the Pier and gardens cost 2d.

Sign of the times… a Pier poster from the 1970s.

A stroll along the prom to the Pier and its pavilion in 1900.

Taking the sea air. Donkeys await their riders on a pleasant summer day. The year is not known.

Tents on the beach, boat trips, swing boat rides and, of course, the famous Cleethorpes donkeys. The date is not known.

Taking the waters… an early beach scene.

Oh, they do like to be beside the sea… a busy day at Cleethorpes in the 1950s.

Not an inch to spare. A packed beach on a summer's day in the 1950s.

This machine was used for beach patrol in 1980.

Despite the weather the trains still rolled in. This was the scene on Whit Monday in 1954. It was raining – but some visitors still insisted

n hiring a deckchair for the day.

A bleak shot of the Promenade taken in 1948.

Enjoying the seaside. The picture was probably taken in the 1950s.

The first big influx of visitors of the season. It was Easter and the sun was shining on Cleethorpes, but the date is unknown. It was probably in the late Forties when this picture was taken from Ross Castle.

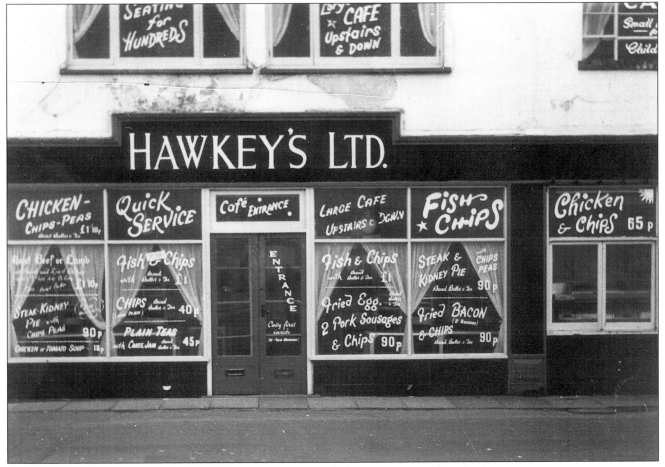

Hawkey's on North Promenade was a popular eating place with the visitors. Note the prices!

Grimsby and Cleethorpes Yachting Club's regatta proved a big attraction for visitors to the resort in July 1950.

Dozens of people queued at Cleethorpes for a special treat – a stick of seaside rock. Taken on the Promenade on June 6, 1949, this picture shows the long wait to be served. Rock, like other sweets, was in short supply because of a sugar shortage.

No shortage in those days. This was Brown's which was situated on the Northern Promenade.

Riding high. The swingboats on the sands were a popular attraction with youngsters. The date is unknown.

The big wheel gave visitors a bird's-eye view of the resort. And a beach stall advertised 'Tea flasks filled'.

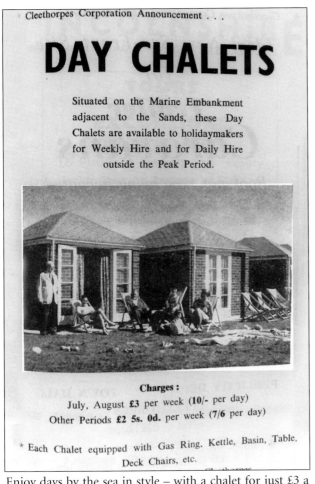

Enjoy days by the sea in style – with a chalet for just £3 a week in the busiest months of the year.

The helter-skelter dominates this beach scene. The date is not known.

Dancing the night away. Youngsters get in the party mood at this event held on the beach at Cleethorpes in 1989.

Taylor's children's roundabout was popular with youngsters in 1912. In the background is another traditional attraction, the helter-skelter.

The Pier approach with Victoria Terrace in the background in the 1920s. The crowds had turned out to see the new sea car, an amphibious vehicle which had the registration number FU 718. It was being paraded to music from a silver band.

Riding the waves. A sea car is put through its paces near the Pier.

One way of looking at it. How many visitors really thought it looked like this as they wound their way back to the station after a good day out?

Over the years the beach at Cleethorpes has seen several unwanted 'visitors' – ships which have run into problems in the river and been washed ashore at the resort. Above is the wreck of the *Sir Henry Havelock* which lay opposite Suggitts Lane.

The hulk of an old lightship ashore at Cleethorpes in April 1955. A plan to convert it into a 'seaside showboat' never came to fruition.

This tank landing craft was washed ashore at Cleethorpes on October 27, 1947 when it was being towed from King's Lynn to Hull for scrapping. The vessel broke in two in heavy seas. The front section went on to Hull but the stern came ashore at Cleethorpes, kept afloat by its watertight bulkheads.

High and dry. Townsfolk inspect a vessel which drifted ashore on the beach in October 1948.

This electronically-detonated mine was British and was washed ashore at Cleethorpes in February 1947.

This was Arcadia which once stood at the 'amusement end' of the promenade opposite Wonderland, an area known years ago as Cleethorpes' Golden Mile. Cleethorpes has never known anything like it – either before or since. The floods of January 31, 1953 left the town devastated, the prom between the Pier and Wonderland being reduced to a shambles. And in the streets of the town, too, there was chaos. A gap had been torn in the sea wall at Suggitt's Lane. Concrete was smashed to pieces. And the lane, as well as Fuller Street and Oliver Street were awash. There was chaos and confusion, too, in Warneford Road, Wilson Street and Manchester Street. And the waters had poured across Grimsby Road, inundating homes as far away as Hart Street and Elliston Street. In Brereton Avenue householders battled against a foot of muddy sea water. Throughout the night people

fought to lift their belongings to the safety of upstairs rooms. On the sea front railway lines were wrecked and fire crews were on constant alert. Chimney stacks collapsed as the gale raged across the town causing fires to break out. It became a night of desperate effort. And the dawn revealed the full scale of the disaster. The attractions which were Cleethorpes' lifeblood were, for the most part, in ruins.

This was Arcadia on January 31, 1953 when the great flood brought devastation to Lincolnshire. Arcadia was built on wooden piles on the beach and was wrecked by the pounding seas which reduced it to matchwood. It was never rebuilt.

Arcadia from the beach – smashed beyond repair.

A workman removes some of the salvagable material from the wreckage of Arcadia.

Victim of the cruel sea… the scene on North Promenade the morning after the 1953 flood. On the left is The Auckland Colonnade and The Gateway cartoon cinema. The wooden wreckage seen here is from the wrecked Arcadia. The car in the picture, an Austin Sheerline saloon, was owned by Sidney Charters Smith, of Brereton Avenue.

Wreckage strewn along the sea front at Wonderland during the floods of 1953. The picture was taken at 9.30pm on January 31.

Wonderland, February 1, 1953.

After the flood… Cleethorpes seafront looking towards Wonderland.

The railway at Cleethorpes following the flood. The picture was taken from the seaward side.

Repairing the Pier entrance.

Grimsby Road under water. The picture was taken at 9.30pm on January 31, 1953.

Spraying cement on to the flood- damaged sea wall at Cleethorpes with a compressed air gun.

Looking at a winter Wonderland. Ice and snow cover the beach in this chilling scene taken in January 1987.

The threat of the tide is well illustrated in this picture of Sea Bank Road – now Kingsway. It was taken in 1902 from opposite the site of the Lifeboat Hotel.

Snow clearance. The beach scene in February 1979.

Snow and ice covers the beach in January 1954.

Heavy seas smash against the sea defences in this wintry scene from January 1954.

The bleak outlook on March 2, 1954 when the beach was covered in snow and ice.

Cleethorpes Council officials inspect damage on the Promenade following stormy weather in October 1990. Left to right are maintenance officer Neal Rothwell, director of technical services Terry Pearce and his deputy, Geoff Cooke.

Youngsters go sledging on Cleethorpes beach following heavy snow in January 1987.

Walking on the water… the scene at the ice-covered Cleethorpes Boating Lake in the harsh winter of 1947. The month was February.

The old Cliffs looking South

The Gardens, Kingsway

Before and After Kingsway was built, Cleethorpes

Looking North

The changing front at Cleethorpes is well illustrated on this old postcard showing the scene before and after the building of Kingsway.

Most visitors never knew of the existence of these greenhouses which stood behind the Promenade attractions. The picture dates back to 1986.

Happy Days

Who remembers… the Café Dansant?

The much-loved venue WAS Cleethorpes for many hundreds of people who danced their nights away to the romantic sounds of big bands.

It began life as the Kingsway Pavilion, once described as 'a delicious Edwardian confection of cast iron, glass and polished floor' and was built for concerts both amateur and professional as well as dancing classes and exhibitions. But in the 1920s the popularity of the type of variety it was built for started to wane and under the Perritt brothers of Grimsby the Pavilion was renamed Café Dansant and became a dance hall.

Wartime saw it increase in popularity and although slightly damaged by bombing it stayed open. A short closure came in 1954 when it was dark and silent for three months, eventually re-opening in style, with guests including Julie Andrews and Alfred Marks.

But the versatility finally ran out and in 1961 it was demolished. The memories, however, still linger for many people.

In November 1985 Mrs G. Hutchinson, of Grimsby, wrote to the *Evening Telegraph* with her memories of the Café Dansant, saying she recalled Mrs Wilkie behind the bar serving coffee, tea and soft drinks. It was 'only sixpence to enter fairyland.' Special requests were played every Sunday afternoon, she said, and Al Bowley was a favourite. Mrs Hutchinson added: 'The Dansant or 'Glass House' as some people called it, was the centre of many romances and a number of young girls had a crush on Tommy Hopkins who played the piano in full evening dress.'

There are many fond memories, too, of The Winter Gardens, built as the Olympia, an amusement hall and restaurant on land formerly known as The Orchard. The man behind the scheme was a well-known figure in Cleethorpes, Mr G. W. Eyre, of Fearnlea, 348 Grimsby Road who was said to be 'seen daily about the streets in his motor bath chair in which he has covered long distances at comparatively high speeds.'

Over the years the Winter Gardens became best known for the internationally famous Melody Night. Company reps from across the north were said to head for the resort for it.

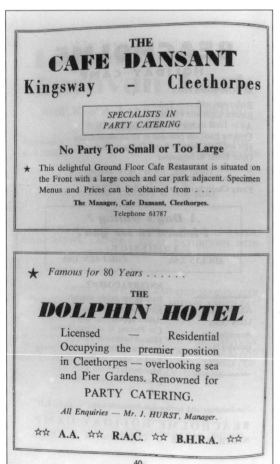

Fred Bury had fond memories of the Café Dansant. He met his wife there and never forgot their first meeting. When the café was demolished he made sure he retained this reminder of it in his garden on Laceby Road.

'Delightful…' a description of the Café Dansant that met with the full agreement of its patrons.

Kings Road, Cleethorpes showing the Winter Gardens (left) and Café Dansant on the right. Trolley bus wires are seen on both sides of the road.

The Dolphin Gardens have for years been a haven of peace and rest for both visitors and residents alike. In recent times it was suggested that they should be turned into a car park providing 45 spaces, but the gardens were saved in 1995 after protests by residents. This picture shows the site of the gardens before they were developed. It was taken in February 1948.

Taking shape… work on the Dolphin Gardens is seen here as it progressed in April 1948.

Phew! With thousands of visitors like this times were good for the owners of the seafront attractions. This picture shows the scene in August 1953. At that time people from Grimsby could travel to the beach on the bus for 5d.

Among the attractions was the model village, parts of which are seen here. A council workman is pictured putting the roof on one of the houses. The village was laid out in the Pier Gardens. The year – 1950.

Cleethorpes has long been renowned for its gardens and floral displays. This one, a tribute to the Royal Naval Association, was created in 1979.

For decades the donkeys on Cleethorpes beach remained a firm favourite with visitors young and old. Over the years several families have run the donkey rides – among them the Appleyards, Crooks, Clarks and, of course, the Nuttalls. Animals owned by the Nuttall family were giving rides before World War One, with Ernie, Albert and Johnnie looking after the business in those days. More recent times saw former Mayor of Cleethorpes Gladys Nuttall and her husband continuing the business. But times on the beach have changed as Mrs Nuttall was to recall in 1996: 'Years ago you would go down to Cleethorpes railway station every day and see how many trains were arriving that day. There would be 10, 20 or 30 trains a day. There would be a Barnsley week, a Sheffield week, a Huddersfield week and so on. Big factories would close down for a week or a fortnight during the summer and people would come to places like Cleethorpes because it was the nearest.' This picture reflects those days and was probably used on a postcard.

Here we go… sailors with the Royal Navy enjoying a day in Cleethorpes in the 1940s.

Gladys Nuttall tends her beloved donkeys, a picture taken in 1985.

Horses and donkeys await riders – a picture from April 1969.

It was the amusement centre for the future – a fun palace which could cater for 20,000 patrons. The *Evening Telegraph* of March 31, 1926 tells of a glorious moment in the story of a Cleethorpes legend. '…East Coast Amusements Ltd have constructed a huge hall at the north end of the Promenade which houses all manner of pleasure giving novelties. The scheme has involved an expenditure of £30,000 and has provided work for over 100 men. The scheme entailed pulling down the 'Dip the Dips' and other erections. The 'Dip the Dips' has now been reconstructed. The main hall is 400ft long and 140ft wide. Inside the hall will be many kinds of amusements and it will be possible for the visitor to spend the full day under cover. In the construction of the hall 3,530 tons of steel, 60 tons of corrugated iron and 28 tons of glass have been used. The whole building is lighted by electricity developed in a power house attached to the hall. The painting of the hall has necessitated the using of 30cwt of paint, blue and white.'

Welcome to Wonderland.

Get ready… this view was a familiar one for the thousands of visitors who rode the Big Dipper at Wonderland as the carriage started its fast descent.

Visitors pack Wonderland on a busy summer's day.

An attraction at the pets' corner at Wonderland were two kangaroos which were tame enough to take food offered to them. The year is not known.

Penguins from Germany were among the attractions at Wonderland at Easter 1953.

Fans battle to meet *Coronation Street* stars Johnny Leeze, of Cleethorpes, Nigel Pivaro and Michael LeVell when they visited Wonderland in 1985.

Staff were dressed for the part when they lined up to be photographed in front of this Wonderland attraction in the 1920s.

A jumble of girders rises into the air as work progresses on erecting the Mad Mouse ride on Cleethorpes seafront in the 1970s.

The end of the Big Dipper in September 1974…

…And this is how it was.

Something for everyone – and admission was free to Hancock's Palace of Pleasure.

Union Jacks flutter in the breeze in this sea front picture from 1906. In the background is the Revolving Tower.

The switchback, forerunner of the roller coaster, which offered thrills to visitors in the early years of the century. This picture is believed to date back to 1904.

Taking shape… the Leisure Centre, which is now a firm favourite with residents and visitors to the seafront, in December 1981.

Olympic champion swimmer Duncan Goodhew pictured during his speech at the opening of the Leisure Centre in January 1983.

Youngsters await the moment when they can try out the Leisure Centre pool for the first time.

A new look for the Paddling Pool. John McNaughton-Jones, contractor Roy Sylvester, Councillor Brian Smith, Councillor Norman Cole and Cleethorpes deputy director of technical services Geoff Cooke at the pool in 1990.

The scene when the old open air bathing pool was being built at Cleethorpes. The idea of having a pool was first put forward in the 1920s. When built it cost £32,000. The pool was badly affected by flooding in 1976 and 1978 and was formally closed because of the dangers to public safety. The council then backed plans to build a leisure centre with a pool.

Enjoying the water at the bathing pool in August 1953.

Youngsters at the bathing pool in August 1962.

The Boating Lake at Cleethorpes offers more than boats. For years it has been a favourite spot with anglers as well as for those who just want to enjoy the scenery. This picture shows visitors enjoying the springtime sunshine at the lake at Easter 1949.

New fish are introduced into the Boating Lake in 1992. Seen here are the council's marketing, promotions and publicity officer, David Wood (left) and John Smith, of the National Rivers Authority.

Enjoying the peace…
a fine picture of the
Boating Lake taken in
November 1948.

Lead poisoning posed
a problem for wildlife
at the Boating Lake in
1984. Here swans
receive treatment
after being affected.

Fun on the lake in April 1952.

Workmen remove an island from the lake in 1975.

Plenty to smile about. Chris Shaw, managing director of the Cleethorpes Light Railway, poses with the steam loco *Sian* who joined her sister engine *Katie* on the tracks in 1995. The engine came to the resort after her owners visited a railway gala in 1994 and were so impressed that they sent her on loan. *Sian* was built in 1963 and was first run on a railway in Wales.

Civic leaders try out the train at Cleethorpes at the start of another holiday season. The date is unknown.

The miniature railway has long been a Cleethorpes attraction. Here Boating Lake supervisor Ken Garratt prepares the engine for the summer season in 1977.

This all-electric miniature railway and station was built by Mr A. Clethro and replaced an earlier steam train which ran along the foreshore. The date is not known.

The butterfly garden formed part of the Jungle World attraction. Here civic leaders see some of the exhibits in the pool area during a tour in 1987.

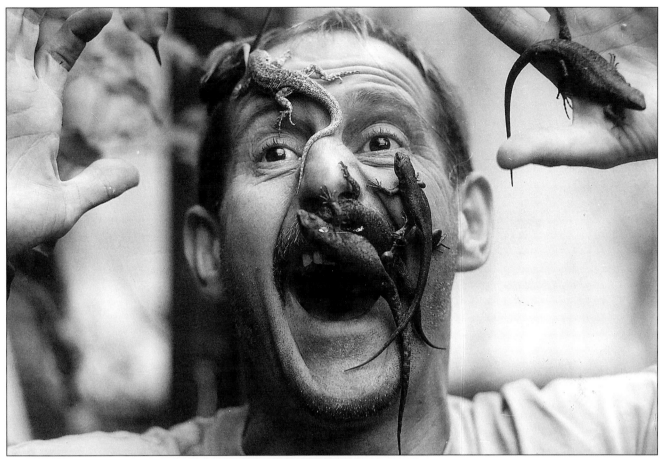

Ugh! Ralph Fitchett, of Jungle World, meets some of the residents.

March 1989 saw the opening of the bowling alley at Cleethorpes. Here partners John Harris (left) and Keith Woodcock toast the project's success.

Thorpe Park is now one of the biggest caravan sites to be found anywhere in Europe. Part of the extensive layout is seen in this 1992 picture.

Miss Thorpe Park Gala Queen 12-year-old Sarah Whittington, receives her sash from general manager of Thorpe Park Gordon Allison in 1994.

Having a splashing time… the Mayor of Cleethorpes, Councillor Keith Brookes, tries out the pool at Thorpe Park in August 1992.

The sea front lights have always been a popular sight with visitors. This display stood the test of time for many years and is seen here in the 1951 display.

…And here it is again – 28 years later in 1979 when the lights were turned on.

One of the set pieces is put into position for the 1966 illuminations.

Lighting up the summer sky. A fine display at Cleethorpes, but the year is not known.

Carnival Time

It's the biggest event in the annual calendar in Cleethorpes. And it is claimed to be one of the biggest events of its kind anywhere in Europe. Cleethorpes Carnival is a major attraction that sees thousands of visitors and residents packing the streets on a Friday evening. The carnival has been a part of life in the resort for decades, as the date on the cover of this programme proves.

Belles of the carnival parade – Miss Cleethorpes Carnival Allison Keeble (second left), Carnival Maid of Honour Laurel Mortimore (left), Carnival Princess Sophie Cowper and Miss Grimsby Evening Telegraph, Yvette Driver in their landau in the 1994 parade.

The carnival parade weaves its way along the sea front – the scene in 1979.

Cleethorpes Amateur Dramatic Society wave to the crowd from their float in the 1978 carnival parade.

Having a great time… crowds along the route of the 1984 parade.

Jamie Bampton (left), of Grimsby, had not planned to enter the competition to be Cleethorpes Carnival Princess until her aunt Lorraine Jensen read about it in the *Evening Telegraph*. When Jamie took the plunge she won and attended various events throughout the carnival week. Seen with her here is Lindsay Walton who the same year – 1989 – beat 22 other contestants to be the maid of honour.

Ingrid Smart travels the route in style in 1988.

The punk look as seen at the 1987 parade.

Happy days… youngsters at the 1990 carnival.

Cleethorpes Carnival Princess in 1980, 13-year-old Cherie Horsewood (left) is seen here after being presented with her trophy by the Mayor, Councillor Mrs Sheila Skane-Davis, (second from left). Looking on are the Maid of Honour, eight-year-old Georgette Desertiaux and the other judges, Mrs Violet Oslear and the Mayor's Consort, Mr Bill Skane-Davis.

A touch of Hawaii in the 1979 carnival parade.

Ooh Aaah… the rustic look formed the style for these participants in the 1979 parade.

Far left: Ooh-la-la. Putting on the style in the big parade.

Left: Winning smiles from the victors in the 1983 carnival waitresses race.

The parade winds its way along the front in 1982.

About Town

The Cleethorpes coat of arms. In September 1936 following a public inquiry Cleethorpes became a borough and was granted a charter signed by King Edward VIII, one of only three which were granted during his short reign. The arms feature two figures, one a Viking, the other a Cleethorpes man named Levi Stephenson, a fisherman whose picture was for many years used on publicity material for the resort.

This special offer marked the granting of the borough's charter.

DIP THE DIPS WONDERLAND Up to 7 p.m.	GHOST TRAIN WONDERLAND Up to 7 p.m.	CHAIRA-PLANES WONDERLAND Up to 7 p.m.	MONA RAILWAY WONDERLAND	SLIDE PROMENADE	HELTER SKELTER FORESHORE	ZOO PROMENADE
BOROUGH OF CLEETHORPES **CHARTER CELEBRATIONS** CHILDRENS DAY, 24th SEPTEMBER, 1936.					BUS OR TRAM IN DISTRICT	JOLLY BOAT PALACE OF PLEASURE
BY KIND PERMISSION OF THE OWNERS OF THE SEVERAL AMUSE-MENTS DETAILED HEREON EACH CHILD IS ENTITLED TO ONE FREE RIDE, Etcetera ON GIVING UP THE APPROPRIATE SECTION OF THIS CARD.						CYCLES FORESHORE
CINEMA	PUTTING	TENNIS	BOATING LAKE	BATHING POOL	BAG OF SEA FOAM CANDY FORESHORE	BUS OR TRAM IN DISTRICT

Wonderland was not so wonderful during wartime. This picture shows the building being used for the manufacture of lorries.

Forty years on… April 1985 and workers on the American vehicles assembly line at Wonderland held their first reunion at the Inn on the Park. Left to right (back) are Mr and Mrs Pat Preston, Flo Colling, Myra Telford, Philamena Jenner, Marjorie Holt, Maud Erander, Pearl Dolphin. (Front) organiser Lillian Jackson, Mme Madeline Dely and Pauline Smith. Mme Dely came from Ostend to attend the event.

A packed meeting in Cleethorpes in February 1946 discussed plans to build a war memorial in the town. The result was the building of the Memorial Hall at the foot of Isaac's Hill. The suggestion that a hall should be built rather than a more traditional memorial came from the Mayor, Alderman Major Albert Cox, who had seen action in both wars. The hall, for which there would be a competition among architects, cost £50,000.

A house at the corner of Clee Road and Brereton Avenue being repaired after a wartime attack. A schoolboy was killed in the raid.

Eighty-one years ago a Clee-thorpes council meeting was told that Mr John Carlbom, of Fulstow Hall, had a gift for the town. It was in the form of an ornamental fountain which was to be erected on the Kingsway – and depicted a boy wearing one boot, the other being held in his hand and through which the water percolated. Mr Carlbom gave the statue as a memorial to his two sons who were born where he lived in the Kingsway. The statue was a copy of an original of Italian origin which was eventually taken to Sweden.

Two stories are connected with the statue. One says that the boy was a newspaper seller who was drowned while fishing. The other is that he was an American drummer boy who cared for dying soldiers on the battlefield, bringing back water in his boot.

The Cleethorpes statue has become famous. But it has over the years been accident prone having been broken on numerous occasions and after one attack the boy was left without a head. During the war service-men took delight in knocking off the boy's arm. Each time, though, he was repaired by Mr C. Jackson, of Brereton Avenue.

Where's the boot? This picture was taken after it had been stolen in April 1959.

Brrr! Ice grips the statue in December 1954.

The Boy With the Leaking Boot stands proudly in a seafront pond in 1962.

Stored away… this was the fate of the statue in 1974. It is now situated in the Tourist Information Office in Alexandra Road.

Bottom left: The seafront fountain definitely came off best when this car hit it in 1949. It was eventually demolished in the 1950s.

Bottom right: The fountain as it was. It is seen here in Sea Road in 1900.

A walk along the Prom in more genteel times. The caption to this photograph (date unknown) said: 'Two miles from Grimsby, down the coast, is this much frequented seaside resort. The promenade was built to resist the encroachment of the sea which had gradually undermined and washed away the tall clay cliff.' The promenade was 'surmounted by a substantial iron railing and constitutes a favourite parade and drive for visitors. Cycles of all descriptions, horses, donkeys and carriages may all be hired here and numbers of seats will be found by the visitor not in request of locomotion.'

This windmill stood in Mill Road. The picture was taken in 1900.

Not what it was – with windows broken and a general air of decay the once-proud Victoria Terrace is a sad reminder of its one-time grandeur. This was the scene in June 1978.

The year was 1936. And this was how Cleethorpes welcomed those visitors wealthy enough to be able to travel by car.

A view inside the pumping station at Cleethorpes Golf Course. The year – 1948.

Time to celebrate. This was Cleethorpes Station in 1963, the year of its centenary.

It was June 1949 but there was not a visitor to be seen at the railway station. The reason – a rail strike stopped trains running.

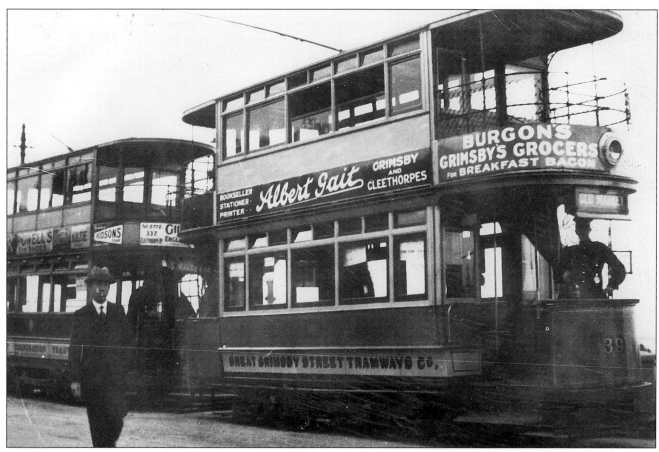

Waiting for their passengers. These trams were pictured at the Kingsway terminus in Cleethorpes in 1926.

Grimsby Road in about 1906.

…And again in the 1920s. The west side of the Cleethorpes end of the road is easily recognised although the picture was taken before all the available house sites had been built on. Note the trees and the central standards which carried tram lines.

Grimsby Road was widened in 1890 and this photograph, looking towards Pelham Road, was taken when the work was in progress, There was no development on the south side of the road at that time. The two large houses on the north side are Stafford House on the west side of Suggitt's Lane and Sunnyside, which was on the east side of the lane.

Workmen busy removing debris at the bottom of Isaac's Hill following the flood of 1953.

Well, what a surprise! Wayne Franks and Barry Westhead discovered this 30ft deep well with 10ft of water below Humber Street in 1988. The well was at the back of Itterby Terrace, which dates back to 1875.

A lone tram winds its way round Isaac's Hill in this picture. The date is unknown.

The old Cleethorpes Library which opened its doors to borrowers in 1901 and served the town for 83 years.

…And the new library which was built by Humberside County Council and opened in August 1984.

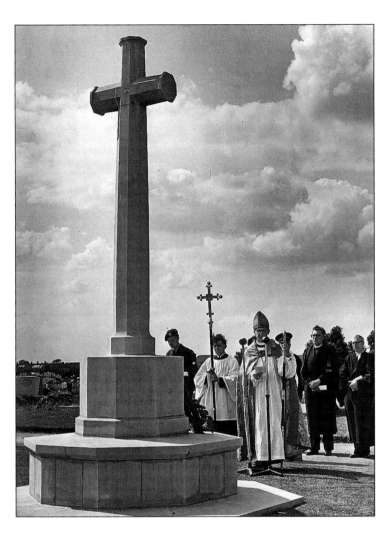

The dedication ceremony for the Cross of Sacrifice erected in Cleethorpes Cemetery. The ceremony took place in July 1951.

The Old Market Place, Cleethorpes in about 1900.

Changing times… a shot of the market taken in 1982.

The Water Tower at Cleethorpes which was demolished in March 1953.

This is one of the best known buildings in Cleethorpes, and one which is instantly recognisable to the tens of thousands of visitors who arrive by road. Built at Isaac's Hill in the 1930s it was for years the offices and showroom of Yorkshire Electricity.

An old view of Alexandra Road showing the tram lines. The date is unknown.

Fresh daily… that was the boast of Knowles Oyster Stores in their seafront shop.

Ye Old Shell Shop had shells, shells and more shells, even being decorated with them as this old picture shows.

Sidney Park has for decades been a popular haunt for residents and visitors alike. This picture shows competitors taking part in a polo match during the Water Rats Gala held there on July 31, 1920.

Some impressive model yachts are seen in this picture of Sidney Park. The date is not known.

A wartime scene on the Sussex Recreation Ground during a demonstration by members of the AFS.

The country park is a 'natural' attraction for residents and visitors. Seen here with the plaque that marks its creation are Councillor Keith Brooks (left), Cleethorpes Borough Council projects officer Duncan Ferguson, the mayor's consort, Bill Parkinson, chief executive Peter Daniel and the Mayor, Councillor Margaret Cracknell.

The Mayor of Cleethorpes, Councillor Mrs Sheila Skane-Davis reads the plaque on a seat donated to Haverstoe Park in 1980. She had officially received the seat from Mrs Alice Hallam (third left) who presented it from all the family in memory of her brother, the late Mr Ken Hopkinson and uncle, Mr Les Hopkinson. Looking on are the Mayor's consort Mr Bill Skane-Davis, family members Mr Alfred Hopkinson, Mrs Alice Hallam, Mr Ernest Curtis, Mrs Louie Hopkinson, Mrs Ivy Hopkinson, the wife of Mr Les Hopkinson, who was a Cleethorpes Parks Department gardener for 20 years, and parks superintendent Mr Jim Patience.

The Mayor, Councillor Margaret Cracknell, Chris Packham and Mayor's Consort Bill Parkinson release ducks into the Boating Lake to officially open the Cleethorpes Discovery Centre in 1995.

A display of rescue work at the drill tower following the opening of the fire station in Cleethorpes by Lord Trent.

It's mopping up time after flooding in St Peter's Avenue in July 1980.

Scaffolding surrounds the Council House during work carried out in 1983. It was built in 1905 and was described as 'a free treatment of English renaissance which has a dignified appearance obtained by a sparing use of ornament and good grouping of the various parts.'

This white cottage, part of a farm, once stood in Cleethorpes Market Place.

The Old Market Place. The date is not known.

Cleethorpes has always been renowned for its floral displays. Sadly this sea front clock was spoiled by vandals in 1977. Borough Council workmen are seen carrying out the repairs.

How many remember the old Cleethorpes Post Office which stood in Yarra Road? The building is now an art centre.

East meets west in Cleethorpes. A totally invisible line ruled to be 'official' over 100 years ago in America, assumes particular importance and interest in Millennium year. The Meridian Line, which separates the Poles and which has been a boon to seamen since the age of sail, is the universal starting point for Longitude which was pronounced internationally acceptable on June 26, 1884 in Washington DC. When the marine embankment was built between Cleethorpes Boating Lake and the dunes at Humberston Fitties in the early 1930s the metal plate was set in the pathway. It was presented by a Sheffield foundry to test a new non-corroding steel.

Marking the Meridian on Cleethorpes seafront.

The year was 1976. This was Tthe scene off Suggitt's Lane as work progressed on sea defences.

The old and the new provide an interesting mixture of styles in this 1990 scene on North Promenade.

Keeping a check on the weather at Cleethorpes Meteorological Station. The year – 1949. The station opened in 1925. Details of temperatures, rainfall and wind speeds were collected and sent to the Met Office, where experts examine data from 319 other similar stations around the country.

It's Showtime

The visit of the *Radio One Roadshow* has become an annual highlight of the year in Cleethorpes – especially for the young. Some of the biggest names in radio make the annual pilgrimage to be met by huge crowds of enthusiastic fans. Typical of the turn-out – and the reaction – is seen here.

Here to entertain you. The Radio One DJ's who toured with the *Roadshow* in 1988.

Singer Michelle Gayle in action during the 1993 *Roadshow* in Cleethorpes.

Cleethorpes here we come. DJ Janice Long pictured at the 1991 event.

Just the ticket. Enthusiastic fans at the 1991 *Roadshow*.

Packing 'em in… the scene at the 1987 *Roadshow*.

Fan-tastic. Peter Powell greets his young supporters in July 1985.

Cleethorpes 'starred' in the BBC's hit programme *It's a Knockout* in 1978. Here compere Stuart Hall introduces another game.

We've won! celebrating success in the 1978 competition.

A cheque for £100 is presented to the Cleethorpes *It's a Knockout* team by Mr Don Beardsley (second left), a partner at G. M. Barton estate agents. Receiving it is team member Ann Petherbridge. Looking on are team members (left to right) Sue Brocklesby, Terry Tuplin, Steve Moses, Brian Swaine and Julie King. The date – August 1978.

The *It's a Knockout* team in 1978.

Training for the *It's a Knockout* competition in 1982.

Cheers!

The colourful frontage of JD's nightclub is a familiar sight in Cleethorpes. The building has seen many changes over the years. This picture shows it as it was originally when it was the Cliff Hotel. The hotel had 'up to' 14 bedrooms each with a sea view, 10 lock-up garages and open air parking for a further 50 cars. The Cliff was advertised as having 'a particularly attractive dining room with small tables and a delightful and spacious lounge.' The pub next door to The Cliff is the Nottingham Hotel. When this picture was taken it sold Gilmour's Ales. It now sells Tetley's.

The Cliff became The Talk of the Town and then The Toby Inn, its owners deciding to create the atmosphere of a Swiss-style chalet with special behind-the-bar features against a backdrop of plastic mountains. The changes began in the 1970s.

The Toby then became Deans, the nightclub being named after the late actor James Dean. It is now JD's. Here late night revellers queue to enter in 1993.

The Queen's Hotel on the corner of Sea View Street and Cambridge Street. The date is unknown.

Some maintained it was the best pub that Cleethorpes ever had. But today the Cross Keys is only a memory. It stood for 170 years on High Street until it was demolished in 1984 for a road widening scheme. This picture shows the pub as it was in 'the good old days'.

Almost gone… the scene at the Cross Keys when the demolition men moved in.

End of an era… Relief landlady Mabel Baskcomb pulls pints for the last time as the Cross Keys closed.

The Clee Park Hotel, pictured here in 1914/15, became Grimsby's first isolation hospital during a smallpox epidemic of 1871 at a cost of admission of £1 a week, a price which led to the number of takers being small. The hospital closed the following year. Over the years the Clee Park built up a loyal clientele. When it closed in 1990 the most loyal of all was Evelyn Butterill who had been a regular for 45 years. She went to the pub every night at 9pm for her pale ale from her home in Taylor Street. "I've seen eight gaffers come and go and everyone treated me well. But the present one, Mike Duffield, really is a great gaffer," she said. And for Evelyn a night at the pub was a real family affair. "It's not every pub that you see your daughters and grandchildren walk in and join you for a drink," she said.

The Clee Park was a popular port of call with fans going to Grimsby Town's Blundell Park ground which is of course within the Cleethorpes boundary, a fact reflected in the pub's sign.

Almost a memory. A picture taken in October 1990 when demolition men razed the pub to the ground.

The Nottingham in Sea View Street is a traditional pub strongly supported by a loyal band of regulars. In this picture drinkers from an earlier age line up for the camera. The date is unknown.

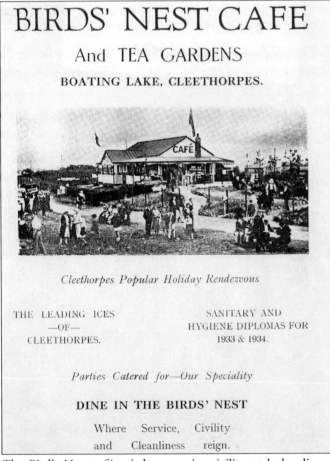

BIRDS' NEST CAFE

And TEA GARDENS

BOATING LAKE, CLEETHORPES.

Cleethorpes Popular Holiday Rendezvous

| THE LEADING ICES
—OF—
CLEETHORPES. | SANITARY AND
HYGIENE DIPLOMAS FOR
1933 & 1934. |

Parties Catered for—Our Speciality

DINE IN THE BIRDS' NEST

Where Service, Civility and Cleanliness reign.

The Bird's Nest café – 'where service civility and cleanliness reign' – at the height of its popularity. The building stood on the site of a former gun emplacement.

The boarded up Bird's Nest Café in 1986.

And this is what replaced it. The Pavilion opened in December 1986 on the café site. Here the management prepare for opening night with tea and a toast. Seen left to right are chef Jim Hayton, proprietors Michael Johnson and Paul West and restaurant manager Alan Cheetham.

This was the ever popular No 1 at Cleethorpes Station in April 1992.

And this was the way the pub looked four years later.

Bill Parkinson brought a new attraction to Cleethorpes when he opened a brewery in the resort. He also opened Willy's Wine Bar and featured annual beer festivals. Seen here at the seventh event held in 1995 is Mr Parkinson (centre) with regulars Dennis Randall and Jonathan Chapman plus manager Paul Hanson with staff members Kay Green and Sharon Lingard preparing to pull the pints.

Robotic boxing helped pull in the punters at The Submarine. Here fists fly as John Tasker (left) and Carl Gaundman take to the ring in 1992.

The only club in the area catering for 'rockers' – that was the proud claim of the Purple Onion in Cleethorpes Market Place. But the club was a short-lived enterprise after hooligans caused damage estimated at £350 in August 1969. A café which formed part of the premises remained open, however. The state of the club is clearly seen in these pictures.

Dancing the day away. These disco dancers took part in a 12-hour sponsored dance session in March 1984 in aid of the campaign to fight muscular dystrophy. The event was held at Strides nightclub. Left to right are Mike Hawkey, Melaney Bailey, Lisa Boden, Lorraine Green, Liz Lewis and Joannie Peterson.

The stars came out at the Pier 39 nightclub in September 1985. Seen here are (rear, left to right) Jane Hazlegrove (Sue Clayton, of *Coronation Street*); Johnny Leeze (Harry Clayton, in *Coronation Street*); Diana Davies (Mrs Bates in *Emmerdale Farm*); Pier owner Mark Mayer; Michael LeVell (Kevin Webster in *Coronation Street*); front, Pam and Ian Sharrock (Jackie Merrick in *Emmerdale Farm*); Willie Morgan (ex-Manchester United and Scotland footballer); Mark Mayer's mother, Rita; and John Stokes, of The Bachelors singing group.

That's Entertainment

It was THE Cleethorpes venue. And the stars thought so, too. Bunny's Place was a dream come true for its owner, former trawler skipper Bunny Newton who took a former bowling alley and bingo hall in Grant Street and converted it into one of the major entertainment venues in the North.

It began in May 1975 when comedian Frankie Howerd stepped onto the newly-constructed stage to make a piece of local entertainment history. The following four years saw some of the biggest names in international showbusiness come to town. Eartha Kitt, Charles Aznavour, Norman Wisdom, Tommy Cooper, Del Shannon, Billy Fury, The Hollies and Bob Monkhouse were just a few of the scores of artists who entertained at Bunny's Place.

The venue, which cost £250,000 to create, was large and could cater for 1,000 people at any one time. Bunny Newton loved the glamour of it all and said: "We got in the top six variety clubs in the country and both Bruce Forsyth and Tommy Cooper said we were in the top three. It was the biggest headache I have ever had, but I loved every minute of it."

Artists commanded big fees which could be anything from a few hundred pounds to £6,000 or £7,000. One singer who did not appear was Shirley Bassey, whose demands were too much for Bunny. She wanted £25,000 for one night, a share of the box office receipts and a 26-piece orchestra. In the end the cost of artists proved too high and led to the closure of Bunny's Place. It was sold to London promoter Alan Goldshaker on May 23, 1979.

May 1975 saw the opening of Bunny's Place with an appearance by Frankie Howerd seen here enjoying a drink with Bunny Newton.

The spacious interior of Bunny's Place.

Behind the scenes… looking after the sound system is Mr Todd.

A shot of the upstairs foyer at Bunny's Place.

The man behind it all. Former skipper Bunny Newton
pictured aboard the Grimsby-registered trawler, *Brandur*.

The stage is set for the opening night's performance at what was to become one of the top entertainment venues and one which
was highly rated by the stars who played there.

American star Eartha Kitt pictured during rehearsals at Bunny's in October 1975.

This was how it ended. The burned out shell of what had been Bunny's Place, which later became Peppers and Shakers night clubs. The fire occurred in 1982.

Saluting a job well done. Workers celebrate at the 'topping out' party following extensions to the Winter Gardens in 1978.

Nights of nostalgia have proved popular at The Winter Gardens. Here the band gets in the mood during an event in May 1983.

The summer of 1937 saw the opening of The Ritz cinema in Cleethorpes, an occasion which was later to bring back memories for Violet Balderson, who had worked as an usherette in the old Lyric in Victoria Street, Grimsby. Over 50 years later she was to recall: 'The foyer of The Ritz was packed with flowers and the beautiful chandeliers were ablaze with light. Milling about the foyer were dozens of celebrities.' Music from the Compton organ was an important part of evenings at The Ritz. Standing by the instrument is organist Noel Briggs. The picture was taken on the opening night – July 31, 1937.

The exterior of The Ritz, on Grimsby Road, Cleethorpes. It was owned by Union Cinemas. The date is unknown. When the Ritz opened Cleethorpes had two other picture houses, the Empire and The Royal, the Coliseum having closed. It was for many years the only place in Cleethorpes with the exception of the Pier Pavilion which could accommodate visiting shows or major orchestral concerts.

All dressed up. Children pictured at a fancy dress party held in The Ritz. The actual date is unknown, but the event is believed to have been held not long after the World War Two.

The Ritz became the ABC in 1956 and still operated under that name when it closed in November 1982.

The last picture show. And the sign, quoting the caption at the end of a Merry Melodies cartoon, says it all.

Steven Putland and Josephine Riley collect two of the last tickets from cashier Mrs Peggy Ayers.

The end. The Ritz vanishes in a pile of rubble in March 1993. McDonald's now occupies the site.

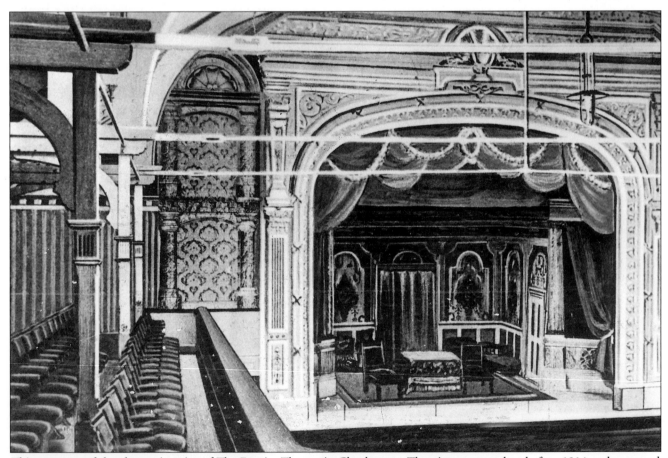

This was part of the elegant interior of The Empire Theatre in Cleethorpes. The picture was taken before 1914 and was used on a postcard.

Sign of the times. The glamour of the stage has gone. The Empire, seen here in 1983 became a bingo hall.

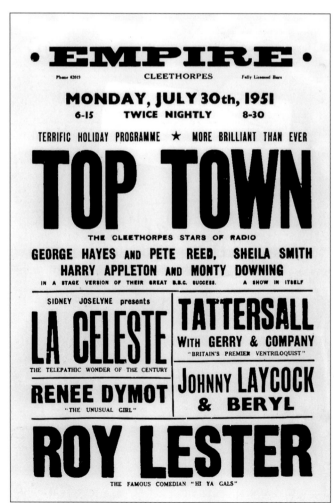

Cleethorpes' success in the *Top Town* competition on radio was reflected in this poster for the Empire when they received star billing.

It was a day when Cleethorpes became famous across the nation. The year 1951 saw a team from the town reach the final of the BBC talent show, *Top Town*. Initially 12 teams from all over the country had taken part and the final was a regional battle with Cleethorpes against Hull. Cleethorpes emerged the winners. The team members were impressionist Harry Appleton, singers Monty Downing and Sheila Smith and comedy duo Pete Reed and George Hayes. As part of the prize they gave a gala broadcast from Cleethorpes and this took place at The Pier on Monday, September 3.

Four hundred free tickets were available and local people queued up to get them, with more than 500 waiting in line by the time the Information Centre in Sea Road opened its doors. On the big night the team was joined by Barney Colehan, who produced the series, and judges Doris Arnold, Jonah Barrington and John Beaumont. Doris presented a scroll to the Mayor, Councillor Cyril Shaw. The broadcast was followed by a civic reception.

Later that year the team was top of the bill at the Empire Theatre in Cleethorpes. But the success story was not to be repeated. The following year Cleethorpes came second to Rochdale – in the first round of the competition.

Winners' smiles from members of the victorious Cleethorpes *Top Town* team as they listened to the radio broadcast of their contest with a team from Hull. Left to right are Pete Reed, George Hayes, Sheila Smith and Harry Appleton.

The Mayor and Mayoress of Cleethorpes in 1951, Councillor and Mrs Cyril Shaw, are seen here at the civic reception for the *Top Town* team. Doris Arnold is seated between them. Others in the picture include the victorious team, the judges and bandleader Ray Martin.

The old Royal Cinema in Grant Street, Cleethorpes. After being demolished it was replaced by a bowling alley and later a night club.

This was all that remained of the Royal in Cleethorpes after it was destroyed by fire in August 1919. It was rebuilt in 1921. The Royal originally opened in 1912 with a film called *Bessie's Ride* and apart from a break during World War One when it was used to billet soldiers, and in the aftermath of the fire, it was a popular attraction until its closure in July 1963.

The Pier Pavilion, probably photographed in the late 1940s or '50s for use on a postcard.

Some of the big names of the entertainment world have appeared in Cleethorpes over the years. Here skiffle king Lonnie Donegan signs up to appear in Startime 80 alongside Clodagh Rodgers and Mike Newman. Seen with him are his agent Roy Hastings on the left and the resort's publicity officer Cameron Watt.

Jack Smethurst of TV's *Love Thy Neighbour* pictured helping to paint the sign for the pantomime *Jack and the Beanstalk* at The Pier in 1980.

Another Pier favourite was Charlie Williams, pictured with the cast of a successful summer season show in 1986.

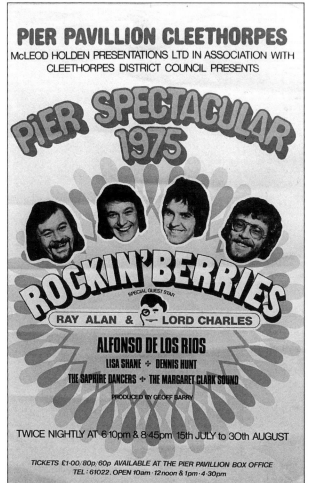

The Nolan Sisters were a big attraction at The Pier in 1979.

Top of the Pops… The Pier Pavilion was a major venue for both residents and visitors. And the Rockin' Berries were still one of the biggest stage acts in the country when they came to Cleethorpes in 1975.

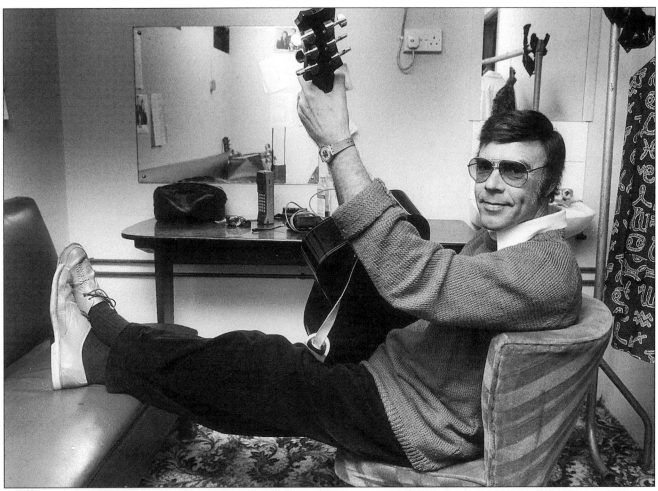

Veteran rock 'n' roll singer Marty Wilde takes it easy before going on stage at the Beachcomber in Humberston in 1989.

The girl in the middle was to become a major name in world entertainment both on the stage and the big screen. She is Julie Andrews, pictured here during a visit to the Café Dansant in Cleethorpes. She appeared with her parents, Ted and Barbara, in 1954.

All lined up and ready to perform for the visitors. These entertainers took part in the pierrot show in 1911.

The Memorial Hall has a long tradition of providing top-flight entertainment. This is the building as it was in 1960.

To commemorate a visit by Ken Dodd to the Memorial Hall the Mayor, Councillor Margaret Cracknell presented him with a framed print. Also pictured are (from left) the Mayor's Consort, Councillor Bill Parkinson, council Chief Executive Peter Daniel, Deputy Mayor Councillor Len Taylor and Deputy Mayoress Councillor Joy Banks.

Wrestling was a popular event in the Memorial Hall. This bout took place in 1988.

Irish singer Val Doonican packed the Memorial Hall when he appeared there in 1994. Pictured with the 'full' sign are staff members Nicola Stark, Hannah Rowley and Amanda Iggo.

Enjoying Life

The show goes on for these members of the popular Cleethorpes entertainers The Edwardians. The picture was taken in 1984.

Youngsters put on the style for their display during the Folk Festival in May 1971.

Dancing in the street and dressed for it, too, during the 1971 Folk Festival.

Entertainers during the 1979 Folk Festival.

Competitors line up ready for the off in the Cleethorpes Fun Run in 1993. Mayor, Coun Kelly Bradley sends them on their way.

Pinching pintas. Daley the bear helps himself to a drink delivered by milkman Dave Grainger when Gandey's Circus was in Cleethorpes in 1984.

It's a circus life for me, said Joanne Lee when she gave up her job in Cleethorpes information office to join Gandey's. Joanne was swept off her feet by high wire motorbike rider Andy Passfield, who she married. At the circus she trained as a trick rider on horseback.

Philip and Carol Gandey pictured before one of their popular summer shows in Cleethorpes in 1989.

Crazy Week brings competitors from all over the North. And it's also popular with local youngsters, too. Here Darren Paine, from Cleethorpes, is seen in the cream cracker eating contest. The year – 1991.

The eyes have it with these Crazy Week competitors in 1989.

Competitors in Crazy Week's Buster's Mighty Joker competition in 1985.

Easy does it for these contestants in the waitresses race during Carnival Week in 1980.

Cleethorpes Band members pictured during a contest in 1984.

Proud owners and their dogs at a show in Cleethorpes in January 1987.

Cleethorpes Ladies Choir in 1992.

Cleethorpes Band members in 1989.

Members of Cleethorpes and County Canine Association and their pets in 1984.

Together again. The year was 1990 and (from left) Mo Hodge, Peggy Hurst, Norah Moyne, Jesse Robinson and Mary Hoyles joined Ken Hoyles, Ernie Drinkall, Bill Green, Dave Robinson and Gordon Mumby for the 20th reunion of the Cleethorpes Cuties at the Winter Gardens.

The Cuties pictured at Christmas in 1983.

The Cleethorpes Cloggies
in action on the seafront
in May 1983.

Cleethorpes String Orchestra pictured at a concert in the Central Hall, Grimsby. The date is not known.

Cleethorpes fire brigade in its early days. The date is unknown.

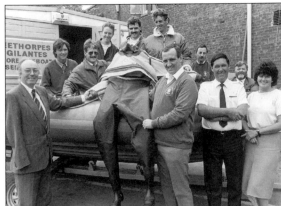

Members of The Vigilantes inshore lifeboat service. The picture was taken in 1990.

Workers at Cleethorpes Gas Works in about 1913.

The start of a big day out. A picture taken as Cleethorpes Methodists left on their outing in 1910.

Young morris dancers pictured at the Pier in about 1911.

Participants in the May Festival of 1937.

Seaside fun from years ago.

The 1963 Gala Queen — Carole Fletcher

Finalists in one of the Summer Contests

The Mayor of Cleethorpes presents the Trophy to Maid of Honour Victoria Osborne, of Sheffield

Cleethorpes is famous for its Beauty Parades!

Contestants in the Princess Parade

A beautiful place to be – how Cleethorpes advertised its beauty parades.

Singing star Clodagh Rodgers (right) *Coronation Street's* Len Fairclough (actor Peter Adamson), Lonnie Donegan and George Kerr are among those pictured with the Mayor of Cleethorpes, Councillor Mrs Sheila Skane-Davis and winning contestants in the 1980 Miss Cleethorpes contest.

The year was 1982 and here comedian Charlie Williams joins Martin Westoby to congratulate the winner of the Miss Cleethorpes title, Jacqui Smith. Also pictured are Susan Hanson (right) who came second and Lydia Sarah Taylor, third.

Rod Hull and Emu were among the judges of the 1981 Miss Cleethorpes competition.

Colin Seavill, general manager of the Beacholme, crowns the winner of the 1977 Miss Beacholme competition.

A kiss from Charlie Williams for the winner of the 1978 Miss Cleethorpes title.

Loudest shouter. It was enough to make Nigel Hutchinson cringe when 13-year-old Crazy Week shouting champion Graham Souter, of Cleethorpes, took the title with a 103.5 decibel roar in 1984. Mr Hutchinson helped run the contest and was winner of the title in the first Crazy Week in 1976.

Mrs Ruth Christley, the wife of Cleethorpes' outdoor activities manager, presents the sash to nine-year-old Christine Ward, of Cleethorpes, the winner of heat two of the Carnival Maid of Honour contest at the Pier Pavilion in July 1978. Second was Kerry Johnson (left) and third Amanda West, both aged nine from Cleethorpes.

Competitors in the Miss Cleethorpes competition in July 1989.

The Fabulous Fitties

The Fitties is a part of local heritage. This unique area is loved by those who have holiday homes there – some for 40 years or more – looked upon as a valuable treasure by conservationists and as a unique area of historic interest by others.

The Humberston Fitties are thought to date from the construction of Haile Sands Fort in World War One when huts and pathways were formed on land which was both low-lying and soggy.

In the 1920s the first plots were leased for the construction of holiday chalets by the farmer who owned the land. And because the land was so low lying many of the buildings on it were built on stilts or piers. In the 1930s the land was bought by the Humberston Fitties Company which in 1938 sold it to Grimsby Rural District Council.

In World War Two soldiers occupied the area, building a radar station and an anti-aircraft position on the site now occupied by the Humber Mouth Yacht Club. The soldiers stayed until 1947 when the Fitties again became a holiday centre.

Today the Fitties is encircled by caravans which started to use the area in the 1950s and 1960s. The Fitties was designated a conservation area in 1990 because of its particular character and historic interest.

How they see The Fitties:
'They are extremely interesting... the chalets are little gems,' – leading architectural photographer Richard Bryant.

'The residents of The Fitties are absolutely superb. Some have been at the site for 40 years,' Councillor Mrs Margaret Solomon, September 1994.

'The Humberston Fitties has survived the seemingly relentless pressure for change and modernisation that has swept away so much of our modern history or consigned it to theme parks of museums. The Fitties is a rare and thriving example of its kind, full of individuality and ingenuity. I was charmed by the place.' Actress Julie Christie.

'A lot of similar places across the country have vanished, while this remains a place of character.' Alfreda Ellidge, Fitties Preservation Society secretary, 1996.

'Every bungalow is very personal. People have a wonderful level of involvement in their own architecture, often including nailing down the boards themselves.' Local architect Rex Critchlow.

A proper little palace... a typical scene on The Fitties in the 1990s.

All neat and tidy on The Fitties.

The chalets on The Fitties in 1987.

This sea wall, known as 'The Pioneer' was built at Humberston Fitties in 1964.

Work on sea defences at The Fitties in 1958.

Humberston Happenings

Besides The Fitties, Humberston is also the home of the ever-popular Beacholme holiday camp. Here, in the snow, guests are seen as they leave after a five month 'occupation'. They are policemen who were moved to the site in 1984 during the miners' strike. The operation cost £800,000 and accommodation was provided for 8,645 men. During their stay they ate nearly 18,000 meals and used 33,000 gallons of petrol in travelling to and from picket lines in Yorkshire. The picture was taken in January 1985.

Rock 'n' roll at the Beacholme. These guests were getting back to the 1950s at one of the special events at the camp.

This was once a Humberston landmark. The 300-year-old thatched cottage was pictured in 1965.

Youngsters attending the Humberston Play Scheme in August 1978.

Before… Field Cottage, Humberston, its tiled roof stripped bare to reveal thatch below, pictured on January 15, 1985.

After… The remains of Field Cottage on January 21, 1985.

The Revd Rodney Owen prepares for Humberston Methodist Church's 75th anniversary in October 1982.

Humberston Church Choir members line up for the camera in 1980.

Preparing for action. Humberston lifeguards receive a new trailer for their rescue boat in March 1977.

They're off… competitors in the Humberston Half Marathon pictured in May 1985.

A Right Royal Welcome

Signing in. The Queen signs her name in the visitor's book during a visit to Cleethorpes in 1958 as Prince Philip and the Mayor, Councillor W. Solomon, look on.

Flags fly and crowds line St Peter's Avenue to greet the royal visitors on June 28, 1958.

The royal car arrives at the Council House.

The Queen enters the Council House with the Mayor and Town Clerk, Mr Gilbert Sutcliffe.

The Queen and Duke meet Ald and Mrs James Magee at Cleethorpes Council House.

The royal visitors meet Mr Arthur Ingham, publicity manager for Cleethorpes, and his wife during their visit to the Council House.

Following their visit the Queen and Duke leave town along St Peter's Avenue.

Watching the royal procession at Isaac's Hill.

Nice to see you… Princess Alice, Duchess of Gloucester, meets local people while on a visit to Cleethorpes in 1985. As Deputy Colonel-in-Chief she was attending the Second Battalion, the Royal Anglian Regiment's celebrations to mark the 300th anniversary of the Royal Lincolnshire Regiment. Princess Alice arrived in a helicopter of the Queen's Flight which landed on the King George V playing field off Taylor's Avenue.

A day to remember… Laura Harmer, a member of 4th Cleethorpes (St Peter's) Brownies meets Princess Alice, who is seen here with the Rector of Cleethorpes, the Revd Brian Wisken. Laura presented the Princess with a posy.

Princess Alice arrives at St Peter's Church with Major-General Sir Christopher Welby-Everard.

Days at the Zoo

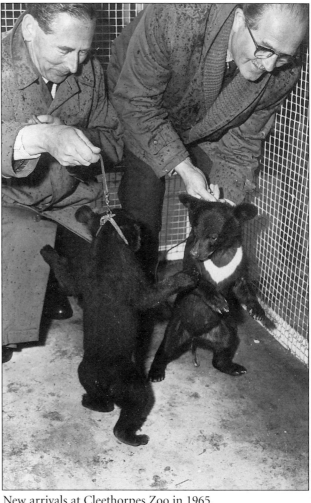

For many visitors a visit to Marineland and the Zoo was an essential part of a day out in Cleethorpes. Both are now long gone, the site now being occupied by the Pleasure Island theme park. This picture from August 1970 sees one of the inhabitants getting a helping hand from the Mayor and Mr Jimmy Jackson.

New arrivals at Cleethorpes Zoo in 1965.

Up and over… zoo assistant Anne Winkie puts one of the dolphins through its paces. The date is unknown.

Trying out the wishing well in June 1970.

Marineland and the Zoo in 1965 bore little resemblance to a major tourist attraction.

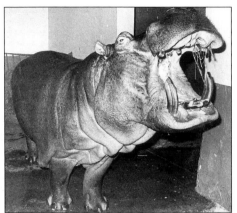

Mrs Betty Verlaine, trainer, and Sparky the chimp check out a forthcoming attraction at the zoo in July 1977.

Hercules the hippo made the headlines in 1979. He arrived at Cleethorpes Zoo from Belle Vue in Manchester but proved too expensive to keep and was threatened with the death sentence. Then in stepped Peggy Manns who declared: "They'll have to shoot me before they shoot Hercules." Mrs Manns raised £6,000 to keep Hercules alive. He was eventually given a new home by Dudley Zoo – and was waved off by 4,000 people.

Making Hercules happy. Supporters turn out to help save the hippo.

The smile of success from Mrs Peggy Manns.

The long and the short… stiltsman George advertises a dolphin show in August 1971.

Easy does it… plastic exhibits arrive on the site in 1994.

Sparky the monkey lays his money on the line to start the Cleethorpes Guide Dogs for the Blind Association's mile of pennies on the Promenade in July 1977. Also pictured are (kneeling) Mr Bernard Bale and Mrs Bet Verlaine, the zoo's managing director and director respectively and (left to right, standing) the association's branch chairman, Mrs B. Atkin; secretary, Mr Les Owens; Mr D. Dawe (committee), Mr J. Landrey with his dog, Miles, Mr Frank Johnson with Tara and Mr Mike Sullivan (committee).

Big smiles from Bernard Bale as he clowns around at the Zoo in May 1978.

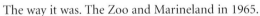

The way it was. The Zoo and Marineland in 1965.

On the move at the zoo in 1977.

Derelict. The zoo in 1983.

Leisure Park staff try out one of the rides in this 1985 picture.

The zoo site has seen many attractions over the years. Many will remember the Leisure Park which occupied the site for some time. Among the attractions was an aviary seen here in May 1984, which had to close after attacks by vandals.

Open at last. Youngsters race to be first through the gates when Pleasure Island opened them for the first time in 1993.

Changing times and changing attractions. The scene from the top of a roller coaster ride at the new Pleasure Island theme park. The picture was taken in 1992.

Bird's-Eye View

Cleethorpes Town Hall, council offices and St Peter's Avenue are clearly seen in this dramatic air view.

How the seagulls see us. In this view coming in over the Pier, the Dolphin Hotel and gardens dominate the foreground. Although cars line up along the seafront the beach is almost clear of people!

The Leisure Centre and King's Road feature in this picture. Note the Boating Lake bottom right.

A fine aerial shot of The Dolphin Hotel. Bottom right is the Clifton Bingo Hall.

The Pier dominates the foreground of this 1983 picture. Opposite is the Pier Hotel. The keen eye can also make out the features of St Peter's Church, while Cleethorpes Market is in full swing in the Market Place. Just off the promenade on the right is the putting course which was built on part of the Dolphin Gardens. Opposite the top of Sea Road is the old Empire Bingo Hall. On the extreme left is part of the former Yarra Road car park which was used for the new Cleethorpes Library. The large building in the centre of the picture is the Boots store in St Peter's Avenue.

Wonderland photographed from the air in 1966.

Cleethorpes out of season. A deserted beach and bathing pool are featured in this shot, which was taken in December 1960.

The bathing pool dominates this picture which was taken in 1965.

Perfect weather helped the photographer with this shot of the Dolphin Hotel in 1965.

The site of Cleethorpes Zoo taken in 1964.

The sun was out and so were the crowds on Whit Monday Bank Holiday in 1964.

A view of the Boating Lake taken in 1961.

The year was 1993 and Pleasure Island was preparing for its first season. The terrifying Boomerang ride is seen on the right. Buck Beck can be seen bounding the development at the bottom of the picture with King's Road at the top.

Chapman's Pond, ever popular with anglers and wildlife alike, was created in the last century by men working for Mr Walwyn Chapman. The site was a brickyard and the present pond was the site from which the raw material (boulder clay) was excavated. It is said that Mr Chapman excavated too deeply and hit a number of chalk springs, being forced to spend a lot of money to plug the gap, but nature won through and the yard had to close. Fish from Abbey Farm, Ludborough, were added in 1919. This picture was taken in 1985.

Around the Churches

Structural weaknesses forced the closure and demolition of Corpus Christi Church, which was built in Cleethorpes in 1930. This picture, taken in 1995, shows work well underway on the new £310,000 hexagonal building which has replaced it. The church, on Grimsby Road, can seat 200 people.

Contractors pictured with Corpus Christi's bell tower before it was lifted into place. Left to right are Allen Tacey, Dave Would, Brian Staples and Alan Bradley.

The old Corpus Christi falls to the demolition men.

A procession moved from the site of the old Corpus Christi to the new church when it was opened.

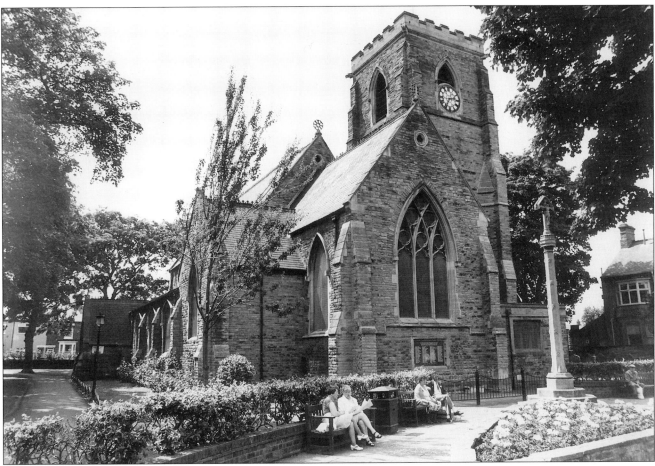

Peace in the heart of town… a pleasant scene at St Peter's Church.

The old Bethel Mission, Tiverton Street in 1981.

Inside the old Bethel Mission. The picture was taken in December 1965.

Miss Elaine George and Mr Peter Alderson who were the first couple to be married at St Andrew's Methodist Church in Cleethorpes. Also pictured is the Revd John Young, the minister. The date – January 1980.

The Minister, the Revd John Young showing members and guests round the new St Andrew's Methodist Church. Left to right are Mr D. A. Bellamy, Miss E. Ingham, Mrs M. Ross, Mrs F. Ingham, Mr Young, Mr C. Craggs, Mr and Mrs H. A. Twydell, Mr and Mrs F. W. Humberstone.

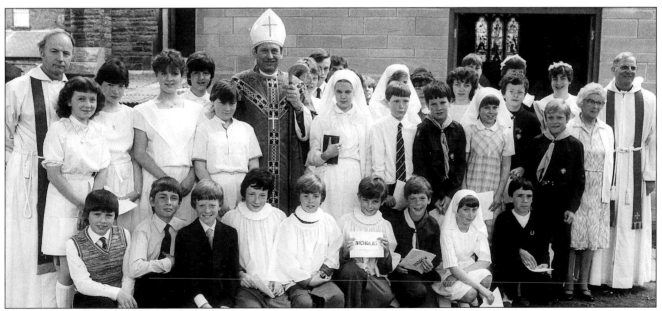

The Bishop of Grimsby, the Rt Revd David Tustin (centre), the Rector of Cleethorpes, the Revd Bryan Wisken (left) and the Revd Vernon Pearcy (right) with the 33 candidates after their service of confirmation at St Peter's Church, Cleethorpes. The picture was taken in 1984.

This Sporting Life

It's been a favourite pub quiz question for years – which team does not play matches in its home town? Why Grimsby Town, of course. Blundell Park has been the home of the Mariners throughout the century and in recent times has seen dramatic changes. This picture shows the ground and its stands as they were in 1960.

Blundell Park in 1984.

The Pontoon Stand has been a part of Blundell Park tradition from the beginning. The original dated back to 1900 and was replaced in 1961 and paid for by the supporters. Many fans will remember the stand as it is seen here having since been demolished and rebuilt in 1995.

A little piece of local – and football history – lies in this picture which shows Mariners fans in the Pontoon Stand for the last time. The stand was demolished because of new all-seater stadium laws.

The year was 1989 and the star of Grimsby Town matches was Harry Haddock as these supporters demonstrate.

Stock car racing was once a big attraction in Cleethorpes. This was one of the events held in 1985.

The annual Easter egg race at Cleethorpes Garden Stadium prior to a race meeting. Pace car driver Malcolm Butler fights a losing battle against enthusiastic youngsters racing to claim the 15 prizes on offer.

An action shot from March 1985.

One of the runners in an August 1984 race.

Place your bets… bookie George Kane was among visitors to the Cleethorpes dog racing track in August 1984.

Bookies line up at the dog track.

That's the way to do it… off-track action before the race.

A competitor manoeuvres round obstacles in the Poacher car rally held on the seafront. The year is not known but the picture is thought to date back to the 1960s.

Some Famous Faces

For more than 35 years Shirley King and Jack Lawton were 'Mr and Mrs Cleethorpes Entertainment'. It was a love affair with a town that they first came to in 1960. Jack had played on the Pier as summer season organist and Shirley arrived for an audition, appearing before what was later described as 'a dour corporation panel'. She got the job. The couple married in 1963 and Shirley, who became pregnant that same year, thought that having a baby, plus the fact that traditional variety shows were in decline, meant her career was over. Then came an offer from Jimmy Jackson at the Winter Gardens to make her the resident singer. The King and Lawton show was by now really on the road. Shirley went on to become marketing and promotions manager at the Winter Gardens, but never lost her love of appearing on stage. The couple left the resort in 1996 to live in Southport.

The irrepressible Shirley King, accompanied by her husband, Jack, was described as 'the east coast's answer to Vera Lynn'. The couple's nostalgia nights at the Winter Gardens were famous throughout the north.

Shirley on stage with a group of young performers in 1985.

That's the way to do it. Shirley King with competitors in an *Evening Telegraph* contest in 1988.

He was one of the most famous footballers of the 1970s. And today Duncan McKenzie is well known as an after-dinner speaker and TV and radio sports personality. Cleethorpes-born Duncan played over 300 games at professional level and scored over 100 goals. But he never played for the team based nearest his home – Grimsby Town. He played for Nottingham Forest from 1967-74, Leeds United between 1974-76, Anderlecht in 1976, Everton from 1976-78, Chelsea from 1978-79 and Blackburn from 1979-81. Duncan also had two years in America with the Tulsa Roughnecks and Chicago Sting.

Movie star John Hurt moved from Derbyshire to Cleethorpes when he was 12 years old. He is the son of the Revd A. H. Hurt, the former vicar of St Aidan's Church. John's mother qualified as an engineer and he has a sister, Monica and a brother, Michael, who is a Roman Catholic monk. Among Hurt's best-known films are *Midnight Express* (1978), *The Elephant Man* (1980) and *Champion* (1983).

The Revd and Mrs A. H. Hurt pictured in 1962 when Mr Hurt was vicar of St Aidan's.

Harry Appleton began his stage career when still a teenager and became one of the best-loved local entertainers of his generation. He died of cancer at the age of 53 in June 1975. Because he was so popular in the town other artists, headed by George Hayes, staged a commemorative show at the Pier on November 30. Tickets cost 75p each.

He has been one of the best known faces in TV soap – as Harry Clayton in *Coronation Street* and more recently, Ned Glover in *Emmerdale*. Johnny Leeze (pictured on the right) is a Yorkshire man who made Cleethorpes his home in 1969 and has lived in the resort ever since. His career in show business really began when he became compere at the Sands Club in Cleethorpes. Prior to that he was a gas fitter. He is pictured here with well-known Cleethorpes personality Roly Godfrey and with the resort's former 'king of clubs' Mark Mayer (left) who died in 1994. Mr Mayer came to the town from North London in 1978 and launched what was to become an entertainment empire. After opening an amusement arcade on North Promenade he built up McCartney's nightclub and Punchbowl pub, which he sold in May 1985. Then he took what many thought was a gamble with the then dilapidated Pier, spending £300,000 to transform it into the Pier 39 bar, restaurant and nightclub. The successful complex was sold in December 1989 to Whitegate Leisure plc. By then Mr Mayer had opened Russell's in High Street, the club later becoming The Limes. He also owned the seafront nightclub Park Lane, formerly Clouds. Another club Mr Mayer developed and sold was The Spanish Steps on North Promenade. In 1993 Mr Mayer, who was often credited with single-handedly reviving Cleethorpes as a nightspot, bought the Flamingo nightclub which he later sold.

Born in Humberston, Rod Temperton became one of the music industry's living legends. The son of Ida and Leslie Temperton, he lived in Church Avenue during his early years. Educated at Reynolds Street School in Cleethorpes he later studied at Grimsby College before working on computers at the Ross factory. As a professional musician Temperton played keyboards with the group Heatwave which in 1977 had a Number One hit with *Boogie Nights*. The song went on to win the US Annual People's Award for most popular record of the year.

Temperton also wrote the title song and two other tracks for Michael Jackson's *Thriller* album. In 1986 he was nominated for the best musical score award for the song *Miss Ceilie's Blues* and the under-score in Steven Spielberg's film *The Colour Purple*. The following year he won the prestigious Ivor Novello Award for the best film score for *Running Scared*, which took him five months to complete.

Rod Temperton (second right) pictured with Heatwave in 1977.

There's nothing like a dame… and Jimmy Slater proved to be the perfect dame. Born in Leeds, he made his first stage appearance at a Skegness concert party in 1914. His first engagement in Cleethorpes, where he was to make his home, was on the beach five years later. Jimmy, with his stunning dresses, went on to present the famous Super Follies in the resort.

Among his claims to fame was that he gave Grimsby comedian Freddie Frinton his first big break in the show *Soldiers in Skirts*. Later the two did a double act until Freddie branched out on his own. He died of a heart attack in 1968.

Jimmy (right) pictured with Freddie Frinton.

Jimmy Slater's Super Follies at Cleethorpes in 1935. Freddie Frinton is seen second from the right.

The Super Follies troupe in 1936. It started in 1912 at a concert party. And that first appearance led to Edna Keyes becoming one of the most popular pub and club entertainers in the area. Over the years Edna starred countless times at shows in the town, her venues ranging from the beach and Pier to clubs and pubs. In the 1930s Edna was to be seen plugging songs in a demonstration depot on the beach. She would later recall: 'I would sing the song, then the crowds would be offered the chance to buy the sheet music.' This was followed by a spell with Twiddle's Party run by Don Twiddle on the Pier. Don and his band later became resident at the Winter Gardens. In 1952 Edna was a member of the Cleethorpes team competing in the BBC *Top Town* contest. The 1980s saw Edna as compère/entertainer at the Clee Park Hotel each Saturday and Sunday. For many years Edna partnered Grimsby entertainer Bing Beales in a popular mime act which became legendary.

Edna pictured when she sold songs on Cleethorpes beach.

Edna pictured with her stage partner Bing in 1988.

The good old days – entertainer Edna Keyes.